Your baby will be a stylishly adorable cutie-pie while wearing one of these 9 cardigans. And you will be amazed at how quickly you can make them! All are knit with medium weight yarn working from the neck down which eliminates having any seams to sew! From lacy yokes, eyelet patterns, cables and Fair Isle designs, you are sure to find one (or more!) that you simply cannot resist.

LEISURE ARTS, INC. • Maumelle, Arkansas

TABLE OF contents

Cabled Eyelets	4	Waves	28
Eyelet Lace	8	Zig-Zag Lace	32
Fair Isle	12	Striped	38
Hearts	16	General Information	43
Leaves	20	Yarn Information	47
Lattice Lace	24	Meet the Designer	48

4

28

3

CABLED eyelets

■■□□ EASY

SHOPPING LIST

Yarn (Medium Weight)
[7 ounces, 370 yards
(198 grams, 338 meters) per skein]:
☐ 1 skein

Knitting Needles
Circular, 24" (61 cm) length
☐ Size 8 (5 mm) **and**
Double pointed, set of 4
☐ Size 8 (5 mm)
or size needed for gauge

Additional Supplies
☐ Cable needle
☐ Stitch holders - 2
☐ Split ring stitch marker
☐ Stitch markers - 8
☐ Sewing needle and matching thread
☐ $^5/_8$" (16 mm) button

SIZE INFORMATION

Size	Finished Chest Measurement
3-6 Months	21" (53.5 cm)
6-9 Months	23½" (59.5 cm)
9-12 Months	25" (63.5 cm)

Size Note: We have printed the instructions for the sizes in different colors to make it easier for you to find:

• Size 3-6 Months in Blue
• Size 6-9 Months in Pink
• Size 9-12 Months in Green

Instructions in Black apply to all sizes.

GAUGE INFORMATION

In Stockinette Stitch
(knit one row, purl one row),
16 sts and 20 rows = 4" (10 cm)

TECHNIQUES USED

- Adding new sts *(Figs. 4a & b, page 45)*
- YO *(Fig. 9, page 46)*
- K2 tog *(Fig. 10, page 46)*

STITCH GUIDE

CABLE 4 FRONT *(abbreviated C4F)*
Slip next 2 sts onto cable needle and hold in **front** of work, K2 from left needle, K2 from cable needle.

UPPER BODY

Beginning at neck edge and using circular needle, cast on 48{52-56} sts.

Row 1: K6{7-8}, place marker *(see Markers, page 44)*, P4, place marker, K4{5-6}, place marker, P4, place marker, K 12, place marker, P4, place marker, K4{5-6}, place marker, P4, place marker, K6{7-8}.

Row 2 (Right side)**:** Knit across to first marker, YO, slip marker, C4F, slip marker, YO, ★ knit across to next marker, YO, slip marker, C4F, slip marker, YO; repeat from ★ 2 times **more**, knit across: 56{60-64} sts.

Row 3: Knit across to first marker, slip marker, P4, slip marker, ★ knit across to next marker, slip marker, P4, slip marker; repeat from ★ 2 times **more**, knit across.

Row 4 (Buttonhole row)**:** Knit across to first marker, YO, slip marker, K4, slip marker, YO, ★ knit across to next marker, YO, slip marker, K4, slip marker, YO; repeat from ★ 2 times **more**, knit across to last 4 sts, K2 tog, YO, K2: 64{68-72} sts.

Row 5: Knit across to first marker, slip marker, P4, slip marker, ★ knit across to next marker, slip marker, P4, slip marker; repeat from ★ 2 times **more**, knit across.

Row 6: Knit across to first marker, YO, slip marker, C4F, slip marker, YO, ★ knit across to next marker, YO, slip marker, C4F, slip maker, YO; repeat from ★ 2 times **more**, knit across: 72{76-80} sts.

Row 7: K4 (band), purl across to last 4 sts, K4 (band).

Row 8: Knit across to first marker, YO, slip marker, K4, slip marker, YO, ★ knit across to next marker, YO, slip marker, K4, slip marker, YO; repeat from ★ 2 times **more**, knit across: 80{84-88} sts.

Row 9: K4, purl across to last 4 sts, K4.

Rows 10 thru 23{**27-29**}**:** Repeat Rows 6-9, 3{4-5} times; then repeat Rows 6 and 7, 1{1-0} time(s) **more** (see Zeros, page 44): 136{156-168} sts.

LOWER BODY

Row 1 (Dividing row)**:** Removing markers, K 20{23-25} (Front), slip next 30{35-38} sts onto st holder (Sleeve), **turn**; add on 4 sts for underarm, **turn**; K 36{40-42} (Back), slip next 30{35-38} sts onto st holder (Sleeve), **turn**; add on 4 sts for underarm, **turn**; knit across: 84{94-100} sts.

Row 2: K4, purl across to last 4 sts, K4.

Row 3: Knit across.

Repeat Rows 2 and 3 for pattern until Lower Body measures approximately 3½{4-5}"/9{10-12.5} cm from underarm **or** ¾" (1.9 cm) less than desired length, ending by working Row 3.

Last 6 Rows: Knit across.

Bind off all sts in **knit**.

SLEEVE

With **right** side facing and using double pointed needle, pick up 4{3-4} sts across one underarm (*Fig. 13, page 46*), place split ring marker around last st picked up to indicate beginning of rnd; slip 10{11-12} sts from st holder onto opposite end of same needle and 10{12-13} sts onto each of 2 empty needles (*Fig. 1, page 44*); knit around: 34{38-42} sts.

Knit each rnd until Sleeve measures approximately 3{4-5}"/7.5{10-12.5} cm from underarm **or** ¾" (1.9 cm) less than desired length.

Next Rnd: Purl around.

Next Rnd: Knit around.

Last 4 Rnds: Repeat last 2 rnds twice.

Bind off all sts in **purl**.

Repeat for remaining Sleeve.

Sew button to band opposite buttonhole.

EYELET *lace*

■■□□ EASY

SHOPPING LIST

Yarn (Medium Weight)
[7 ounces, 370 yards
(198 grams, 338 meters) per skein]:
☐ 1 skein

Knitting Needles
Circular, 24" (61 cm) length
☐ Size 8 (5 mm) **and**
Double pointed, set of 4
☐ Size 8 (5 mm)
or size needed for gauge

Additional Supplies
☐ Stitch holders - 2
☐ Split ring stitch marker
☐ Stitch markers - 8
☐ Sewing needle and matching thread
☐ ⅝" (16 mm) buttons - 3

SIZE INFORMATION

Size	Finished Chest Measurement
3-6 Months	20" (51 cm)
6-9 Months	22½" (57 cm)
9-12 Months	24" (61 cm)

Size Note: We have printed the instructions for the sizes in different colors to make it easier for you to find:

• Size 3-6 Months in Blue
• Size 6-9 Months in Pink
• Size 9-12 Months in Green

Instructions in Black apply to all sizes.

GAUGE INFORMATION

In Stockinette Stitch
(knit one row, purl one row),
16 sts and 20 rows = 4" (10 cm)

TECHNIQUES USED

- Adding new sts (Figs. 4a & b, page 45)
- YO (Fig. 9, page 46)
- K2 tog (Fig. 10, page 46)

UPPER BODY

Beginning at neck edge and using circular needle, cast on 48{52-56} sts.

Row 1: K8{9-10}, place marker (see Markers, page 44), K1, place marker, K8{9-10}, place marker, K1, place marker, K 12, place marker, K1, place marker, K8{9-10}, place marker, K1, place marker, K8{9-10}.

Row 2 (Right side): Knit across to first marker, YO, slip marker, K1, slip marker, YO, ★ knit across to next marker, YO, slip marker, K1, slip marker, YO; repeat from ★ 2 times more, knit across: 56{60-64} sts.

Row 3: Knit across.

Row 4 (Buttonhole row): Knit across to first marker, YO, slip marker, K1, slip marker, YO, ★ knit across to next marker, YO, slip marker, K1, slip marker, YO; repeat from ★ 2 times more, knit across to last 4 sts, K2 tog, YO, K2: 64{68-72} sts.

Work buttonhole at end of every 10th row twice.

Row 5: Knit across.

Row 6: Knit across to first marker, YO, slip marker, K1, slip marker, YO, ★ knit across to next marker, YO, slip marker, K1, slip marker, YO; repeat from ★ 2 times more, knit across: 72{76-80} sts.

Row 7: Knit across.

Row 8 (Increase row): Knit across to first marker, YO, slip marker, K1, slip marker, YO, ★ knit across to next marker, YO, slip marker, K1, slip marker, YO; repeat from ★ 2 times more, knit across: 80{84-88} sts.

Row 9: K4 (band), purl across to last 4 sts, K4 (band).

Rows 10 thru 23{27-29}: Repeat Rows 8 and 9, 7{9-10} times: 136{156-168} sts.

LOWER BODY

Row 1 (Dividing row): Removing markers, K 20{23-25} (Front), slip next 30{35-38} sts onto st holder (Sleeve), **turn**; add on 4 sts for underarm, **turn**; K 36{40-42} (Back), slip next 30{35-38} sts onto st holder (Sleeve), **turn**; add on 4 sts for underarm, **turn**; knit across: 84{94-100} sts.

Row 2: K4, purl across to last 4 sts, K4.

Row 3: Knit across.

Rows 4 and 5: Repeat Rows 2 and 3.

Row 6: Knit across.

Row 7: K4, (K2 tog, YO) across to last 4 sts, K4.

Rows 8-10: K4, purl across to last 4 sts, K4.

Row 11: Knit across.

Row 12: K4, purl across to last 4 sts, K4.

Row 13: Knit across.

Rows 14-26: Repeat Rows 6-13 once, then repeat Rows 6-10 once **more**.

Row 27: Knit across.

Row 28: K4, purl across to last 4 sts, K4.

Repeat Rows 27 and 28 for pattern until Lower Body measures approximately 4¾{5-5½}"/ 12{12.5-14} cm from underarm or ¾" (1.9 cm) less than desired length, ending by working a **right** side row.

Last 6 Rows: Knit across.

Bind off all sts in **knit**.

SLEEVE

With **right** side facing and using double pointed needle, pick up 4{3-4} sts across one underarm *(Fig. 13, page 46)*, place split ring marker around last st picked up to indicate beginning of rnd; slip 10{11-12} sts from st holder onto opposite end of same needle and 10{12-13} sts onto each of 2 empty needles *(Fig. 1, page 44)*; knit around: 34{38-42} sts.

Knit each rnd until Sleeve measures approximately ¾{1¾-2¾}"/1.9{4.5-7} cm from underarm.

EYELET PATTERN

Rnd 1: Purl around.

Rnd 2: (K2 tog, YO) around.

Rnd 3: Knit around.

Rnd 4: Purl around.

Rnds 5-8: Knit around.

Rnds 9-12: Repeat Rnds 1-4.

Knit each rnd until Sleeve measures approximately 3½{4-5}"/9{10-12.5} cm from underarm or ¾" (1.9 cm) less than desired length.

Next Rnd: Purl around.

Next Rnd: Knit around.

Last 4 Rnds: Repeat last 2 rnds twice.

Bind off all sts in **purl**.

Repeat for remaining Sleeve.

Sew buttons to band opposite buttonholes.

FAIR isle

■□□ EASY

SHOPPING LIST

Yarn (Medium Weight)
[2.5 ounces, 121 yards
(70 grams, 111 meters) per skein]:
☐ Grey Multi - 2 skeins
[3.5 ounces, 170 yards
(198 grams, 156 meters) per skein]:
☐ Gold - 1 skein
☐ Red - 1 skein

Knitting Needles

Circular, 24" (61 cm) length
☐ Size 8 (5 mm) **and**
Double pointed, set of 4
☐ Size 8 (5 mm)
   or size needed for gauge

Additional Supplies

☐ Stitch holders - 2
☐ Split ring stitch marker
☐ Sewing needle and matching thread
☐ ⅝" (16 mm) buttons - 5{6-7}

SIZE INFORMATION

Size	Finished Chest Measurement
3-6 Months	20" (51 cm)
6-9 Months	22½" (57 cm)
9-12 Months	24" (61 cm)

Size Note: We have printed the instructions for the sizes in different colors to make it easier for you to find:

• Size 3-6 Months in Blue
• Size 6-9 Months in Pink
• Size 9-12 Months in Green

Instructions in Black apply to all sizes.

GAUGE INFORMATION

In Stockinette Stitch
(knit one row, purl one row),
16 sts and 20 rows = 4" (10 cm)

TECHNIQUES USED

- Adding new sts *(Figs. 4a & b, page 45)*
- Knit increase *(Figs. 5a & b, page 45)*
- M1 *(Figs. 7a & b, page 45)*
- M1P *(Figs. 8a & b, page 46)*
- YO *(Fig. 9, page 46)*
- K2 tog *(Fig. 10, page 46)*

UPPER BODY

Beginning at neck edge, using circular needle and Grey Multi, cast on 48{52-56} sts.

Rows 1 and 2: Knit across.

Boys' Only - Row 3 (Buttonhole row): Knit across to last 4 sts, K2 tog, YO, K2.

Girls' Only - Row 3 (Buttonhole row): K2, YO, K2 tog, knit across.

Work buttonhole every 10th row, 4{5-6} times.

Size 3-6 Months Only

Row 4 (Right side): K4, M1, (knit increase in next 5 sts, M1) across to last 4 sts, K4: 97 sts.

Row 5: K4 (band), purl across to last 4 sts, K4 (band).

Row 6: Knit across.

Row 7: K4, purl across to last 4 sts, K4.

Size 6-9 Months Only

Row 4 (Right side): K5, knit increase in next 2 sts, (M1, knit increase in next 4 sts) across to last 5 sts, M1, K5: 105 sts.

Row 5: K4 (band), purl across to last 4 sts, K4 (band).

Row 6: Knit across.

Row 7: K4, purl across to last 4 sts, K4.

Size 9-12 Months Only

Row 4 (Right side): K4, M1, (knit increase in next 6 sts, M1) across to last 4 sts, K4: 113 sts.

Row 5: K4 (band), purl across to last 4 sts, K4 (band).

Row 6: Knit across.

Rows 7-9: Repeat Rows 5 and 6 once, then repeat Row 5 once **more**.

ALL SIZES - FAIR ISLE STRIPE

Row 1: K4, drop Grey Multi *(Fig. 3, page 45)*; with Gold, knit across to last 4 sts, drop Gold; with second Grey Multi, K4.

Row 2: K4, drop Grey Multi; with Gold, purl across to last 4 sts, drop Gold; with second Grey Multi, K4.

Rows 3-5: Follow Chart on page 15 between bands *(see Following a Chart and Stranding, page 44)*.

Size 3-6 Months Only

Row 6: K4, drop Grey Multi; with Gold, P5, (M1P, P4) across to last 4 sts, drop Gold; with second Grey Multi, K4: 118 sts.

Sizes 6-9 Months & 9-12 Months Only

Row 6: K4, drop Grey Multi; with Gold, (P4, M1P) across to last 5 sts, M1P, P1, drop Gold; with second Grey Multi, K4: {130-140} sts.

ALL SIZES

Row 7: K4, drop Grey Multi; with Gold, knit across to last 4 sts, cut Gold; with second Grey Multi, K4.

Row 8: K4, cut second Grey Multi; purl across to last 4 sts, K4.

Row 9: Knit across.

Size 3-6 Months Only

Row 10: K4, P7, M1P, (P6, M1P) across to last 11 sts, M1P, P7, K4: 136 sts.

Size 6-9 Months Only

Row 10: K4, P1, M1P, (P5, M1P) across to last 5 sts, P1, M1P, K4: 156 sts.

Size 9-12 Months Only

Row 10: K4, M1P, P3, M1P, (P5, M1P) across to last 8 sts, P4, M1P, K4: 168 sts.

ALL SIZES

Row 11: Knit across.

Row 12: K4, purl across to last 4 sts, K4.

Rows 13 thru 24{28-30}: Repeat Rows 11 and 12, 6{8-9} times.

LOWER BODY

Row 1 (Dividing row): K 20{23-25} (Front), slip next 30{35-38} sts onto st holder (Sleeve), **turn**; add on 4 sts for underarm, **turn**; K 36{40-42} (Back), slip next 30{35-38} sts onto st holder (Sleeve), **turn**; add on 4 sts for underarm, **turn**; knit across: 84{94-100} sts.

Row 2: K4, purl across to last 4 sts, K4.

Row 3: Knit across.

Repeat Rows 2 and 3 for pattern until Lower Body measures approximately 4{4½-5}"/10{11.5-12.5} cm from underarm **or** ¾" (1.9 cm) less than desired length, ending by working Row 3.

Last 6 Rows: Knit across.

Bind off all sts in **knit**.

SLEEVE

With **right** side facing and using double pointed needle, pick up 4{3-4} sts across one underarm *(Fig. 13, page 46)*, place split ring marker around last st picked up to indicate beginning of rnd *(see Markers, page 44)*; slip 10{11-12} sts from st holder onto opposite end of same needle and 10{12-13} sts onto each of 2 empty needles *(Fig. 1, page 44)*; knit around: 34{38-42} sts.

Knit each rnd until Sleeve measures approximately 3{4-5}"/7.5{10-12.5} cm from underarm **or** ¾" (1.9 cm) less than desired length.

Next Rnd: Purl around.

Next Rnd: Knit around.

Last 4 Rnds: Repeat last 2 rnds twice.

Bind off all sts in **purl**.

Repeat for remaining Sleeve.

Sew buttons to band opposite buttonholes.

CHART

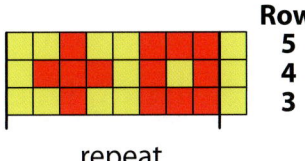

repeat

On **right** side rows, follow Chart from **right** to **left**. On **wrong** side row, follow Chart from **left** to **right**.

hearts

■■□□ EASY

SHOPPING LIST

Yarn (Medium Weight)
[3.5 ounces, 170 yards
(198 grams, 156 meters) per skein]:
☐ Grey - 2 skeins
☐ Red - 1 skein

Knitting Needles

Circular, 24" (61 cm) length
☐ Size 8 (5 mm) **and**
Double pointed, set of 4
☐ Size 8 (5 mm)
  or size needed for gauge

Additional Supplies

☐ Stitch holders - 2
☐ Split ring stitch marker
☐ Stitch markers - 4
☐ Sewing needle and matching thread
☐ ⅝" (16 mm) buttons - 5{6-7}

SIZE INFORMATION

Size	Finished Chest Measurement
3-6 Months	20¼" (51.5 cm)
6-9 Months	23½" (59.5 cm)
9-12 Months	25¾" (66 cm)

Size Note: We have printed the instructions for the sizes in different colors to make it easier for you to find:

• Size 3-6 Months in Blue
• Size 6-9 Months in Pink
• Size 9-12 Months in Green

Instructions in Black apply to all sizes.

GAUGE INFORMATION

In Stockinette Stitch
(knit one row, purl one row),
16 sts and 20 rows = 4" (10 cm)

TECHNIQUES USED

- Adding new sts *(Figs. 4a & b, page 45)*
- Knit increase *(Figs. 5a & b, page 45)*
- YO *(Fig. 9, page 46)*
- K2 tog *(Fig. 10, page 46)*

Roll two small separate balls of Red.

UPPER BODY

Beginning at neck edge, using circular needle and Red, cast on 47{52-55} sts.

Row 1: K8{9-10}, place marker, *(see Markers, page 44)*, K9{10-11}, place marker, K 13{14-13}, place marker, K9{10-11}, place marker, K8{9-10}.

Row 2 (Right side): Knit across to within one st of first marker, knit increase, slip marker, knit increase, ★ knit across to within one st of next marker, knit increase, slip marker, knit increase; repeat from ★ 2 times **more**, knit across: 55{60-63} sts.

Row 3: Knit across.

Boys' Only - Row 4 (Buttonhole row)**:** K2, YO, K2 tog, knit across to within one st of first marker, knit increase, slip marker, knit increase, ★ knit across to within one st of next marker, knit increase, slip marker, knit increase; repeat from ★ 2 times **more**, knit across: 63{68-71} sts.

Girls' Only - Row 4 (Buttonhole row)**:** Knit across to within one st of first marker, knit increase, slip marker, knit increase, ★ knit across to within one st of next marker, knit increase, slip marker, knit increase; repeat from ★ 2 times **more**, knit across to last 4 sts, K2 tog, YO, K2: 63{68-71} sts.

Work buttonhole every 10th row, 4{5-6} times.

Row 5: Knit across.

Row 6: K4, drop Red; with Grey *(Fig. 3, page 44)*, knit across to within one st of first marker, knit increase, slip marker, knit increase, ★ knit across to within one st of next marker, knit increase, slip marker, knit increase; repeat from ★ 2 times **more**, knit across to last 4 sts, drop Grey; with second Red, K4: 71{76-79} sts.

Row 7: K4, drop Red; with Grey, purl across to last 4 sts, drop Grey; with second Red, K4.

Row 8 (Increase row): K4, drop Red; with Grey, knit across to within one st of first marker, knit increase, slip marker, knit increase, ★ knit across to within one st of next marker, knit increase, slip marker, knit increase; repeat from ★ 2 times **more**, knit across to last 4 sts, drop Grey; with second Red, K4: 79{84-87} sts.

Row 9: K4, drop Red, with Grey, purl across to last 4 sts, drop Grey; with second Red, K4.

Rows 10 thru 23{27-29}: Repeat Rows 8 and 9, 7{9-10} times: 135{156-167} sts.

LOWER BODY

Row 1 (Dividing row): Removing markers, K4, drop Red; with Grey, K 16{19-21} (Front), slip next 30{35-38} sts onto st holder (Sleeve), **turn**; add on 4 sts for underarm, **turn**; K 35{40-41} (Back), slip next 30{35-38} sts onto st holder (Sleeve), **turn**; add on 4 sts for underarm, **turn**; knit across to last 4 sts, drop Grey; with second Red, K4: 83{94-99} sts.

Row 2: K4, drop Red; with Grey, purl across to last 4 sts, drop Grey; with second Red, K4.

Row 3: K4, drop Red, with Grey, knit across to last marker working knit increase 2{4-8} times evenly spaced across *(see Increasing Evenly Across a Row, page 45)*, drop Grey, with second Red, K4: 85{98-107} sts.

Row 4: K4, drop Red; with Grey, purl across to last 4 sts, drop Grey; with second Red, K4.

Row 5: K4, drop Red; with Grey, knit across to last 4 sts, drop Grey; with second Red, K4.

Repeat Rows 4 and 5 for pattern until Lower Body measures approximately 2{3-4}"/5{7.5-10} cm from underarm, ending by working a **wrong** side row.

Next 6 Rows: Follow Chart between bands *(see Following a Chart and Stranding, page 44)*.

Next Row: K4, drop Red, with Grey knit across to last marker, drop Grey, with second Red, K4.

Next Row: K4, drop Red; with Grey, purl across to last 4 sts, drop Grey; with second Red, K4.

Repeat last 2 rows for pattern until Lower Body measures approximately 4{5-6}"/10{12.5-16.5} cm from underarm **or** ¾" (1.9 cm) less than desired length, ending by working a **wrong** side row; cut Grey.

Next Row: With Red, knit across, cutting small ball of Red.

Last 5 Rows: Knit across.

Bind off all sts in **knit**.

SLEEVE

With **right** side facing, using double pointed needle, and Grey, pick up 4{3-4} sts across one underarm *(Fig. 13, page 46)*, place split ring marker around last st picked up to indicate beginning of rnd; slip 10{11-12} sts from st holder onto opposite end of same needle and 10{12-13} sts onto each of 2 empty needles *(Fig. 1, page 44)*; knit around: 34{38-42} sts.

Knit each rnd until Sleeve measures approximately 3{4-5}"/7.5{10-12.5} cm from underarm **or** ¾" (1.9 cm) less than desired length; at end of last rnd, cut Grey.

Next Rnd: With Red, purl around.

Next Rnd: Knit around.

Last 4 Rnds: Repeat last 2 rnds twice.

Bind off all sts in **purl**.

Repeat for remaining Sleeve.

Sew buttons to band opposite buttonholes.

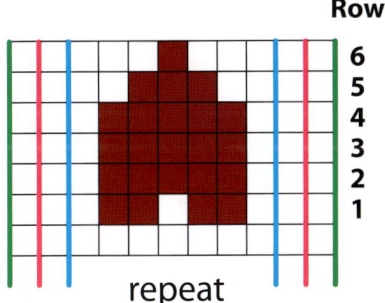

CHART

leaves

 EASY

SHOPPING LIST

Yarn (Medium Weight)
[3.5 ounces, 170 yards
(198 grams, 156 meters) per skein]:
☐ 2 skeins

Knitting Needles
Circular, 24" (61 cm) length
☐ Size 8 (5 mm) **and**
Double pointed, set of 4
☐ Size 8 (5 mm)
  or size needed for gauge

Additional Supplies
☐ Stitch holders - 2
☐ Split ring stitch marker
☐ Sewing needle and matching thread
☐ ⅝" (16 mm) buttons - 5{6-7}

SIZE INFORMATION

Size	Finished Chest Measurement
3-6 Months	20" (51 cm)
6-9 Months	22½" (57 cm)
9-12 Months	24" (61 cm)

Size Note: We have printed the instructions for the sizes in different colors to make it easier for you to find:

• Size 3-6 Months in Blue
• Size 6-9 Months in Pink
• Size 9-12 Months in Green

Instructions in Black apply to all sizes.

GAUGE INFORMATION

In Stockinette Stitch
(knit one row, purl one row),
16 sts and 20 rows = 4" (10 cm)

TECHNIQUES USED

- Adding new sts *(Figs. 4a & b, page 45)*
- Knit increase *(Figs. 5a & b, page 45)*
- M1 *(Figs. 7a & b, page 45)*
- YO *(Fig. 9, page 46)*
- K2 tog *(Fig. 10, page 46)*
- Slip 1, K1, PSSO *(Fig. 11, page 46)*
- Slip 2 tog, K1, P2SSO *(Figs. 12a & b, page 46)*

UPPER BODY

Beginning at neck edge and using circular needle, cast on 48{52-56} sts.

Rows 1 and 2: Knit across.

Row 3 (Buttonhole row)**:** Knit across to last 4 sts, K2 tog, YO, K2.

Work buttonhole at end of every 10th row, 4{5-6} times.

Size 3-6 Months Only

Row 4 (Right side)**:** K4, M1, (knit increase in next 4 sts, M1) across to last 4 sts, K4: 99 sts.

Row 5: K4 (band), purl across to last 4 sts, K4 (band).

Size 6-9 Months Only

Row 4 (Right side)**:** K4, (knit increase in next 4 sts, M1) across to last 4 sts, K4: 107 sts.

Row 5: K4 (band), purl across to last 4 sts, K4 (band).

Row 6: Knit across.

Row 7: K4, purl across to last 4 sts, K4.

Size 9-12 Months Only

Row 4 (Right side)**:** K5, knit increase in next 3 sts, M1, (knit increase in next 4 sts, M1) across to last 4 sts, K4: 115 sts.

Row 5: K4 (band), purl across to last 4 sts, K4 (band).

Row 6: Knit across.

Rows 7-9: Repeat Rows 5 and 6 once, then repeat Row 5 once **more**.

ALL SIZES

Row 6{**8**-**10**}**:** K7, K2 tog, YO, K1, YO, slip 1, K1, PSSO, ★ K3, K2 tog, YO, K1, YO, slip 1, K1, PSSO; repeat from ★ across to last 7 sts, K7.

Row 7{**9**-**11**}**:** K4, purl across to last 4 sts, K4.

Row 8{**10**-**12**}**:** K6, K2 tog, YO, K3, YO, slip 1, K1, PSSO, ★ K1, K2 tog, YO, K3, YO, slip 1, K1, PSSO; repeat from ★ across to last 6 sts, K6.

Row 9{**11**-**13**}**:** K4, purl across to last 4 sts, K4.

Row 10{**12**-**14**}**:** K5, K2 tog, YO, K5, ★ YO, slip 2 tog, K1, P2SSO, YO, K5; repeat from ★ across to last 7 sts, YO, slip 1, K1, PSSO, K5.

Rows 11{**13**-**15**} **thru 13**{**15**-**17**}**:** Repeat Rows 9{11-13} and 10{12-14} once, then repeat Row 9{11-13} once **more**.

Row 14{**16**-**18**}**:** K7, YO, slip 1, K1, PSSO, K1, K2 tog, ★ YO, K3, YO, slip 1, K1, PSSO, K1, K2 tog; repeat from ★ across to last 7 sts, YO, K7.

Row 15{**17**-**19**}**:** K4, purl across to last 4 sts, K4.

Row 16{**18**-**20**}**:** K8, YO, slip 2 tog, K1, P2SSO, ★ YO, K5, YO, slip 2 tog, K1, P2SSO; repeat from ★ across to last 8 sts, YO, K8.

Row 17{**19**-**21**}**:** K4, purl across to last 4 sts, K4.

Size 3-6 Months Only

Row 18: K5, M1, (K3, M1, K2, M1) across to last 4 sts, K4: 136 sts.

Row 19: K4, purl across to last 4 sts, K4.

Row 20: Knit across.

Row 21: K4, purl across to last 4 sts, K4.

Size 6-9 Months Only

Row 20: K5, M1, (K2, M1) across to last 6 sts, K6: 156 sts.

Row 21: K4, purl across to last 4 sts, K4.

Row 22: Knit across.

Rows 23-25: Repeat Rows 21 and 22 once, then repeat Row 21 once **more**.

Size 9-12 Months Only

Row 22: K5, M1, (K2, M1) across to last 6 sts, K6: 168 sts.

Row 23: K4, purl across to last 4 sts, K4.

Row 24: Knit across.

Rows 25-29: Repeat Rows 23 and 24 twice, then repeat Row 23 once **more**.

LOWER BODY

Row 1 (Dividing row)**:** K 20{23-25} (Front), slip next 30{35-38} sts onto st holder (Sleeve), **turn**; add on 4 sts for underarm, **turn**; K 36{40-42} (Back), slip next 30{35-38} sts onto st holder (Sleeve), **turn**; add on 4 sts for underarm, **turn**; knit across: 84{94-100} sts.

Row 2: K4, purl across to last 4 sts, K4.

Row 3: Knit across.

Repeat Rows 2 and 3 for pattern until Lower Body measures approximately 4½{4¾-5}"/11.5{12-12.5} cm from underarm **or** ¾" (1.9 cm) less than desired length, ending by working Row 3.

Last 6 Rows: Knit across.

Bind off all sts in **knit**.

SLEEVE

With **right** side facing and using double pointed needle, pick up 4{3-4} sts across one underarm *(Fig. 13, page 46)*, place split ring marker around last st picked up to indicate beginning of rnd *(see Markers, page 44)*; slip 10{11-12} sts from st holder onto opposite end of same needle and 10{12-13} sts onto each of 2 empty needles *(Fig. 1, page 44)*; knit around: 34{38-42} sts.

Knit each rnd until Sleeve measures approximately 3{4-5}"/7.5{10-12.5} cm from underarm **or** ¾" (1.9 cm) less than desired length.

Next Rnd: Purl around.

Next Rnd: Knit around.

Last 4 Rnds: Repeat last 2 rnds twice.

Bind off all sts in **purl**.

Repeat for remaining Sleeve.

Sew buttons to band opposite buttonholes.

LATTICE *lace*

■■□□ EASY

SHOPPING LIST

Yarn (Medium Weight)
[7 ounces, 370 yards
(198 grams, 338 meters) per skein]:
☐ 1 skein

Knitting Needles
Circular, 24" (61 cm) length
☐ Size 8 (5 mm) **and**
Double pointed, set of 4
☐ Size 8 (5 mm)
   or size needed for gauge

Additional Supplies
☐ Stitch holders - 2
☐ Split ring stitch marker
☐ Sewing needle and matching thread
☐ ⅝" (16 mm) buttons - 3

SIZE INFORMATION

Size	Finished Chest Measurement
3-6 Months	20" (51 cm)
6-9 Months	22½" (57 cm)
9-12 Months	24" (61 cm)

Size Note: We have printed the instructions for the sizes in different colors to make it easier for you to find:

• Size 3-6 Months in Blue
• Size 6-9 Months in Pink
• Size 9-12 Months in Green

Instructions in Black apply to all sizes.

GAUGE INFORMATION

In Stockinette Stitch
  (knit one row, purl one row),
  16 sts and 20 rows = 4" (10 cm)

TECHNIQUES USED

- Adding new sts *(Figs. 4a & b, page 45)*
- Knit increase *(Figs. 5a & b, page 45)*
- M1 *(Figs. 7a & b, page 45)*
- YO *(Fig. 9, page 46)*
- K2 tog *(Fig. 10, page 46)*

UPPER BODY

Beginning at neck edge and using circular needle, cast on 48{52-56} sts.

Rows 1 and 2: Knit across.

Row 3 (Right side - Buttonhole row)**:** Knit across to last 4 sts, K2 tog, YO, K2.

Work buttonhole at end of every 10th row twice.

Sizes 3-6 Months & 9-12 Months Only

Row 4: K4, ★ knit increase in next 10{6} sts, M1; repeat from ★ across to last 4 sts, K4: 92{112} sts.

Size 6-9 Months Only

Row 4: K4, M1, knit increase in next 7 sts, M1, ★ knit increase in next 6 sts, M1; repeat from ★ across to last 11 sts, knit increase in next 7 sts, M1, K4: 104 sts.

ALL SIZES

Row 5: K4, (K2 tog, YO) across to last 4 sts, K4.

Row 6: K4 (band), purl across to last 4 sts, K4 (band).

Row 7: K4, (YO, K2 tog) across to last 4 sts, K4.

Row 8: K4, purl across to last 4 sts, K4.

Row 9: K4, (K2 tog, YO) across to last 4 sts, K4.

Row 10: K4, purl across to last 4 sts, K4.

Size 3-6 Months Only

Row 11: (K4, M1) across to last 4 sts, K4: 114 sts.

Rows 12 and 13: Knit across.

Row 14: K4, (M1, K5) across: 136 sts.

Sizes 6-9 Months & 9-12 Months Only

Row 11: K4, M1, (K1, knit increase) twice, (M1, K4) across: {131-141} sts.

Rows 12 and 13: Knit across.

Row 14: K6, M1, (K5, M1) across to last 5 sts, K5: {156-168} sts.

ALL SIZES

Rows 15-20: Repeat Rows 5-10.

Rows 21-24: Knit across.

Row 25: K4, purl across to last 4 sts, K4.

Sizes 6-9 Months & 9-12 Months Only

Rows {26-26} thru {27-29}: Repeat Rows 24 and 25, {1-2} time(s).

LOWER BODY

Row 1 (Dividing row): K 20{23-25} (Front), slip next 30{35-38} sts onto st holder (Sleeve), **turn**; add on 4 sts for underarm, **turn**; K 36{40-42} (Back), slip next 30{35-38} sts onto st holder (Sleeve), **turn**; add on 4 sts for underarm, **turn**; knit across: 84{94-100} sts.

Row 2: K4, purl across to last 4 sts, K4.

Row 3: Knit across.

Repeat Rows 2 and 3 for pattern until Lower Body measures approximately 4½{4¾-5}"/11.5{12-12.5} cm from underarm or ¾" (1.9 cm) less than desired length, ending by working Row 3.

Last 6 Rows: Knit across.

Bind off all sts in **knit**.

SLEEVE

With **right** side facing and using double pointed needle, pick up 4{3-4} sts across one underarm *(Fig. 13, page 46)*, place split ring marker around last st picked up to indicate beginning of rnd *(see Markers, page 44)*; slip 10{11-12} sts from st holder onto opposite end of same needle and 10{12-13} sts onto each of 2 empty needles *(Fig. 1, page 44)*; knit around: 34{38-42} sts.

Knit each rnd until Sleeve measures approximately 3{4-5}"/7.5{10-12.5} cm from underarm or ¾" (1.9 cm) less than desired length.

Next Rnd: Purl around.

Next Rnd: Knit around.

Last 4 Rnds: Repeat last 2 rnds twice.

Bind off all sts in **purl**.

Repeat for remaining Sleeve.

Sew buttons to band opposite buttonholes.

waves

▮▮▯▯ EASY

SHOPPING LIST

Yarn (Medium Weight)
[7 ounces, 370 yards
(198 grams, 338 meters) per skein]:
☐ 1 skein

Knitting Needles
Circular, 24" (61 cm) length
☐ Size 8 (5 mm) **and**
Double pointed, set of 4
☐ Size 8 (5 mm)
 or size needed for gauge

Additional Supplies
☐ Stitch holders - 2
☐ Split ring stitch marker
☐ Stitch markers - 8
☐ Sewing needle and matching thread
☐ ⅝" (16 mm) buttons - 5{6-7}

SIZE INFORMATION

Size	Finished Chest Measurement
3-6 Months	20¼" (51.5 cm)
6-9 Months	22¼" (56.5 cm)
9-12 Months	24¼" (61.5 cm)

Size Note: We have printed the instructions for the sizes in different colors to make it easier for you to find:

• Size 3-6 Months in Blue
• Size 6-9 Months in Pink
• Size 9-12 Months in Green

Instructions in Black apply to all sizes.

29

GAUGE INFORMATION

In Stockinette Stitch
(knit one row, purl one row),
16 sts and 20 rows = 4" (10 cm)

TECHNIQUES USED

- Adding new sts *(Figs. 4a & b, page 45)*
- Purl increase *(Figs. 8a & b, page 45)*
- YO *(Fig. 9, page 46)*
- Slip 2 tog, K1, P2SSO *(Figs. 12a & b, page 46)*

UPPER BODY

Beginning at neck edge and using circular needle, cast on 49{53-57} sts.

Row 1: K8{9-10}, place marker *(see Markers, page 44)*, K1, place marker, K8{9-10}, place marker, K1, place marker, K 13, place marker, K1, place marker, K8{9-10}, place marker, K1, place marker, knit across.

Row 2 (Right side)**:** Knit across to first marker, YO, slip marker, K1, slip marker, YO, ★ knit across to next marker, YO, slip marker, K1, slip marker, YO; repeat from ★ 2 times **more**, knit across: 57{61-65} sts.

Row 3: Knit across.

Row 4 (Buttonhole row)**:** Knit across to first marker, YO, slip marker, K1, slip marker, YO, ★ knit across to next marker, YO, slip marker, K1, slip marker, YO; repeat from ★ 2 times **more**, knit across to last 4 sts, K2 tog, YO, K2: 65{69-73} sts.

Work buttonhole at end of every 10th row, 4{5-6} times.

Row 5: Knit across.

Row 6 (Increase row)**:** Knit across to first marker, YO, slip marker, K1, slip marker, YO, ★ knit across to next marker, YO, slip marker, K1, slip marker, YO; repeat from ★ 2 times **more**, knit across: 73{77-81} sts.

Row 7: K4, purl across to last 4 sts, K4.

Rows 8 thru 23{27-29}: Repeat Rows 6 and 7, 8{10-11} times: 137{157-169} sts.

LOWER BODY

Row 1 (Dividing row)**:** Removing markers, K 20{22-24} (Front), slip next 30{36-38} sts onto st holder (Sleeve), **turn**; add on 4 sts for underarm, **turn**; K 37{41-45} (Back), slip next 30{36-38} sts onto st holder (Sleeve), **turn**; add on 4 sts for underarm, **turn**; knit across: 85{93-101} sts.

Row 2: K4, purl across to last 4 sts working purl increase 4 times evenly spaced (*see Increasing Evenly Across a Row, page 45*), K4: 89{97-105} sts.

Row 3: K5, YO, K2, slip 2 tog, K1, P2SSO, K2, YO, ★ K1, YO, K2, slip 2 tog, K1, P2SSO, K2, YO; repeat from ★ across to last 5 sts, K5.

Row 4: K4, purl across to last 4 sts, K4.

Row 5: K6, YO, K1, slip 2 tog, K1, P2SSO, K1, YO, ★ K3, YO, K1, slip 2 tog, K1, P2SSO, K1, YO; repeat from ★ across to last 6 sts, K6.

Row 6: K4, purl across to last 4 sts, K4.

Row 7: K7, YO, slip 2 tog, K1, P2SSO, YO, ★ K5, YO, slip 2 tog, K1, P2SSO, YO; repeat from ★ across to last 7 sts, K7.

Row 8: K4, purl across to last 4 sts, K4.

Repeat Rows 3-8 for pattern until Lower Body measures approximately 4¼{5¼-6¼}"/11{13.5-16} cm from underarm, ending by working a **right** side row.

Last 6 Rows: Knit across.

Bind off all sts in **knit**.

SLEEVE

With **right** side facing and using double pointed needle, pick up 4 sts across one underarm (*Fig. 13, page 46*), place split ring marker around last st picked up to indicate beginning of rnd; slip 10{12-14} sts from st holder onto opposite end of same needle and 10{12-12} sts onto each of 2 empty needles (*Fig. 1, page 44*); knit around: 34{40-42} sts.

Knit each rnd until Sleeve measures approximately 3{4-5}"/ 7.5{10-12.5} cm from underarm **or** ¾" (1.9 cm) less than desired length.

Next Rnd: Purl around.

Next Rnd: Knit around.

Last 4 Rnds: Repeat last 2 rnds twice.

Bind off all sts in **purl**.

Repeat for remaining Sleeve.

Sew buttons to band opposite buttonholes.

ZIG-ZAG lace

■■□□ EASY

SHOPPING LIST

Yarn (Medium Weight)
[7 ounces, 370 yards
(198 grams, 338 meters) per skein]:
☐ 1 skein

Knitting Needles
Circular, 24" (61 cm) length
☐ Size 8 (5 mm) **and**
Double pointed, set of 4
☐ Size 8 (5 mm)
or size needed for gauge

Additional Supplies
☐ Stitch holders - 2
☐ Split ring stitch marker
☐ Sewing needle and matching thread
☐ ⅝" (16 mm) buttons - 3

SIZE INFORMATION

Size	Finished Chest Measurement
3-6 Months	20" (51 cm)
6-9 Months	22½" (57 cm)
9-12 Months	24" (61 cm)

Size Note: We have printed the instructions for the sizes in different colors to make it easier for you to find:

• Size 3-6 Months in Blue
• Size 6-9 Months in Pink
• Size 9-12 Months in Green

Instructions in Black apply to all sizes.

GAUGE INFORMATION

In Stockinette Stitch
(knit one row, purl one row),
16 sts and 20 rows = 4" (10 cm)

TECHNIQUES USED

- Adding new sts *(Figs. 4a & b, page 45)*
- Knit increase *(Figs. 5a & b, page 45)*
- M1 *(Figs. 7a & b, page 45)*
- YO *(Fig. 9, page 46)*
- K2 tog *(Fig. 10, page 46)*
- Slip 1, K1, PSSO *(Fig. 11, page 46)*
- Slip 2 tog, K1, P2SSO *(Figs. 12a & b, page 46)*

UPPER BODY

Beginning at neck edge and using circular needle, cast on 48{52-56} sts.

Rows 1 and 2: Knit across.

Row 3 (Right side - Buttonhole row)**:** Knit across to last 4 sts, K2 tog, YO, K2.

Work buttonhole at end of every 10th row twice.

Row 4: Knit increase in each st across: 96{104-112} sts.

Row 5: Knit across.

Row 6: K4 (band), purl across to last 4 sts, K4 (band).

Rows 7 thru 9{9-11}: Repeat Rows 5 and 6, 1{1-2} time(s); then repeat Row 5 once **more**.

Row 10{10-12}: Knit across.

Size 3-6 Months Only

Row 11: K5, M1, (K3, knit increase) across to last 7 sts, M1, knit increase twice, K5: 121 sts.

Size 6-9 Months Only

Row 11: K4, M1, (K3, knit increase) across to last 4 sts, K4: 129 sts.

Size 9-12 Months Only

Row 13: K7, knit increase, (K3, knit increase) across to last 8 sts, K8: 137 sts.

ALL SIZES

Row 12{12-14}: K4, purl across to last 4 sts, K4.

Row 13{13-15}: K5, YO, slip 1, K1, PSSO, K3, K2 tog, YO, ★ K1, YO, slip 1, K1, PSSO, K3, K2 tog, YO; repeat from ★ across to last 5 sts, K5.

Row 14{14-16}: K4, purl across to last 4 sts, K4.

Row 15{15-17}: K6, YO, slip 1, K1, PSSO, K1, K2 tog, YO, ★ K3, YO, slip 1, K1, PSSO, K1, K2 tog, YO; repeat from ★ across to last 6 sts, K6.

Row 16{16-18}: K4, purl across to last 4 sts, K4.

Row 17{17-19}: K7, YO, slip 2 tog, K1, P2SSO, YO, ★ K5, YO, slip 2 tog, K1, P2SSO, YO; repeat from ★ across to last 7 sts, K7.

Row 18{18-20}: K4, purl across to last 4 sts, K4.

Rows 19{19-21} thru 20{21-23}: Knit across.

Size 3-6 Months Only

Row 21: K 11, M1, (K7, M1) across to last 12 sts, K 12: 136 sts.

Row 22: K4, purl across to last 4 sts, K4.

Size 6-9 Months Only

Row 22: K4, purl across to last 4 sts, K4.

Row 23: Knit across.

Row 24: K4, purl across to last 4 sts, K4.

Row 25: K 12, M1, (K4, M1) across to last 13 sts, K 13: 156 sts.

Sizes 9-12 Months Only

Row 24: K4, purl across to last 4 sts, K4.

Row 25: Knit across.

Rows 26-28: Repeat Rows 24 and 25 once, then repeat Row 24 once **more**.

Row 29: K9, M1, (K4, M1) across to last 8 sts, K8: 168 sts.

LOWER BODY

Row 1 (Dividing row): K 20{23-25} (Front), slip next 30{35-38} sts onto st holder (Sleeve), **turn**; add on 4 sts for underarm, **turn**; K 36{40-42} (Back), slip next 30{35-38} sts onto st holder (Sleeve), **turn**; add on 4 sts for underarm, **turn**; knit across: 84{94-100} sts.

Row 2: K4, purl across to last 4 sts, K4.

Row 3: Knit across.

Repeat Rows 2 and 3 for pattern until Lower Body measures approximately 4¼{4¾-5}"/11{11.5-12.5} cm from underarm or ¾" (1.9 cm) less than desired length, ending by working Row 4.

Last 7 Rows: Knit across.

Bind off all sts in **knit**.

SLEEVE

Rnd 1: With **right** side facing and using double pointed needle, pick up 4 sts across one underarm *(Fig. 13, page 46)*, place split ring marker around last st picked up to indicate beginning of rnd *(see Markers, page 44)*; slip 10{11-12} sts from st holder onto opposite end of same needle and 10{12-13} sts onto each of 2 empty needles *(Fig. 1, page 44)*; knit around: 34{39-42} sts.

Rnd 2: Purl around.

Rnd 3: Knit around.

Rnds 4-7: Repeat Rnds 2 and 3 twice.

Bind off all sts in **purl**.

Repeat for remaining Sleeve.

Sew buttons to band opposite buttonholes.

37

striped

EASY

SHOPPING LIST

Yarn (Medium Weight) [4]

[3.5 ounces, 170 yards
(198 grams, 156 meters) per skein]:

- ☐ Blue - 1 skein
- ☐ Lt Blue - 1 skein

Knitting Needles

Circular, 24" (61 cm) length
- ☐ Size 8 (5 mm) **and**

Double pointed, set of 4
- ☐ Size 8 (5 mm)

   or size needed for gauge

Additional Supplies

- ☐ Stitch holders - 2
- ☐ Split ring stitch marker
- ☐ Stitch markers - 4
- ☐ Sewing needle and matching thread
- ☐ ⅝" (16 mm) buttons - 5{6-7}

SIZE INFORMATION

Size	Finished Chest Measurement
3-6 Months	19¾" (50 cm)
6-9 Months	22½" (57 cm)
9-12 Months	23¾" (60.5 cm)

Size Note: We have printed the instructions for the sizes in different colors to make it easier for you to find:

- Size 3-6 Months in Blue
- Size 6-9 Months in Pink
- Size 9-12 Months in Green

Instructions in Black apply to all sizes.

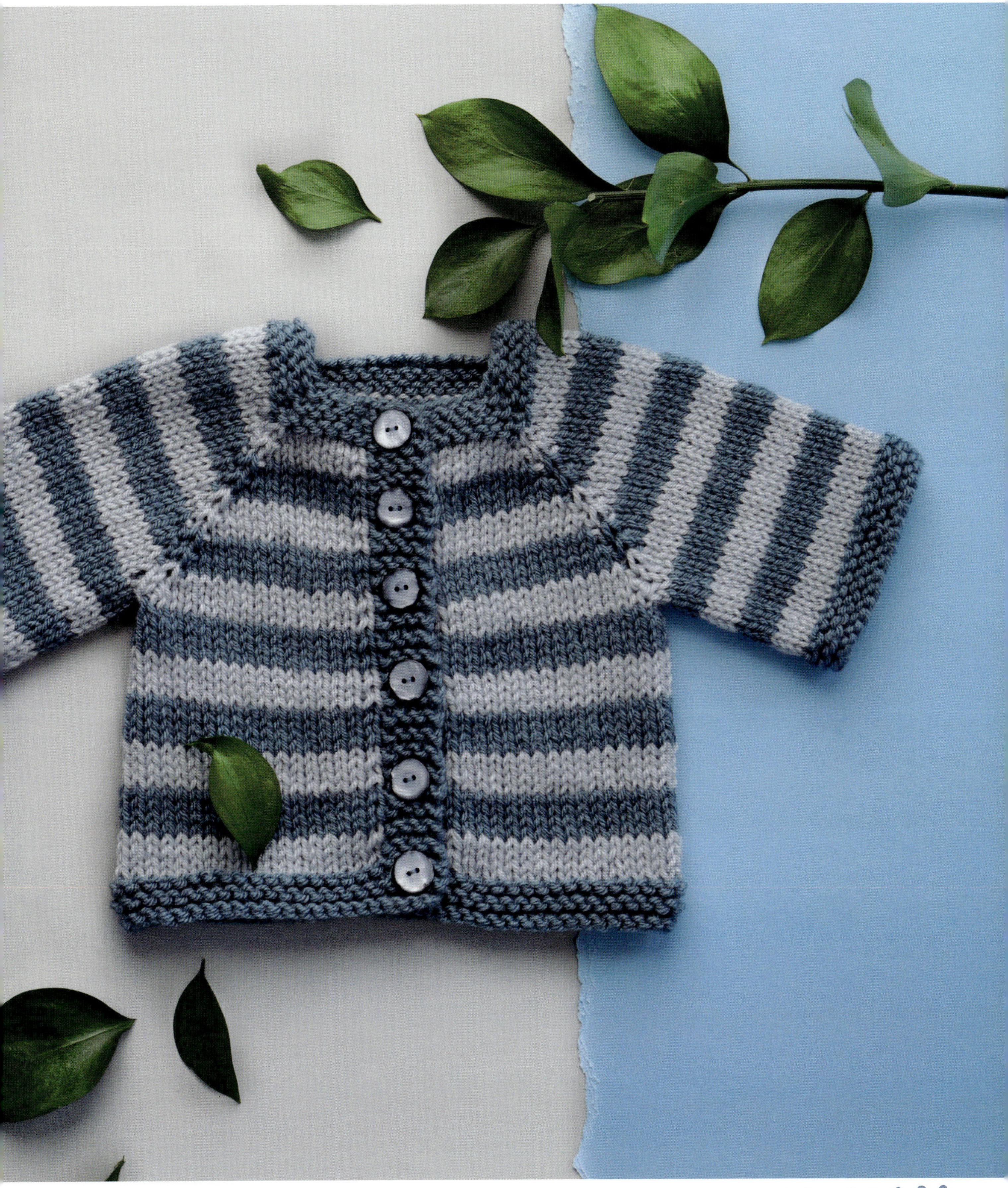

GAUGE INFORMATION

In Stockinette Stitch
(knit one row, purl one row),
16 sts and 20 rows = 4" (10 cm)

TECHNIQUES USED

- Adding new sts *(Figs. 4a & b, page 45)*
- Knit increase *(Figs. 5a & b, page 45)*
- YO *(Fig. 9, page 46)*
- K2 tog *(Fig.10, page 46)*

Roll a small separate ball of Blue.

UPPER BODY

Beginning at neck edge, using circular needle and Blue, cast on 47{52-55} sts.

Row 1: K8{9-10}, place marker *(see Markers, page 44)*, K9{10-11}, place marker, K 13{14-13}, place marker, K9{10-11}, place marker, K8{9-10}.

Row 2 (Right side): Knit across to within one st of first marker, knit increase, slip marker, knit increase, ★ knit across to within one st of next marker, knit increase, slip marker, knit increase; repeat from ★ 2 times **more**, knit across: 55{60-63} sts.

Row 3: Knit across.

Girls' Only - Row 4 (Buttonhole row): Knit across to within one st of first marker, knit increase, slip marker, knit increase, ★ knit across to within one st of next marker, knit increase, slip marker, knit increase; repeat from ★ 2 times **more**, knit across to last 4 sts, K2 tog, YO, K2: 63{68-71} sts.

Boys' Only - Row 4 (Buttonhole row): K2, YO, K2 tog, knit across to within one st of first marker, knit increase, slip marker, knit increase, ★ knit across to within one st of next marker, knit increase, slip marker, knit increase; repeat from ★ 2 times **more**, knit across: 63{68-71} sts.

Work buttonhole every 10th row, 4{5-6} times.

Row 5: Knit across.

Row 6 (Increase row): K4, drop Blue; with Lt Blue *(Fig. 3, page 45)*, knit across to within one st of first marker, knit increase, slip marker, knit increase, ★ knit across to within one st of next marker, knit increase, slip marker, knit increase; repeat from ★ 2 times **more**, knit across to last 4 sts, drop Lt Blue; with second Blue, K4: 71{76-79} sts.

Row 7: K4, drop Blue; with Lt Blue, purl across to last 4 sts, drop Lt Blue; with second Blue, K4.

Row 8 (Increase row): K4, drop Blue; with Lt Blue, knit across to within one st of first marker, knit increase, slip marker, knit increase, ★ knit across to within one st of next marker, knit increase, slip marker, knit increase; repeat from ★ 2 times **more**, knit across to last 4 sts, drop Lt Blue; with second Blue, K4: 79{84-87} sts.

Row 9: K4, drop Blue; with Lt Blue, purl across to last 4 sts, drop Lt Blue; with second Blue, K4.

Row 10 (Increase row): Knit across to within one st of first marker, knit increase, slip marker, knit increase, ★ knit across to within one st of next marker, knit increase, slip marker, knit increase; repeat from ★ 2 times **more**, knit across to last 4 sts, drop Blue; with second Blue, K4: 87{92-95} sts.

Carry unused color loosely along **wrong** side of piece, twisting colors every two rows to prevent long strands. Work 4 rows/rnds of each color throughout, working first 4 sts and last 4 sts (bands) with Blue.

Row 11: K4, drop Blue; with second Blue, purl across to last 4 sts, K4.

Rows 12 and 13: Repeat Rows 10 and 11: 95{100-103} sts.

Size 3-6 Months Only

Rows 14-23: Repeat Rows 6-13 once, then repeat Rows 6 and 7 once **more**: 135 sts.

Row 24: K4, drop Blue; with Lt Blue, knit across to last 4 sts, drop Lt Blue; with Blue, K4.

Row 25: K4, drop Blue; with Lt Blue, purl across to last 4 sts, drop Lt Blue; with second Blue, K4.

Size 6-9 Months Only

Rows 14-27: Repeat Rows 6-13 once, then repeat Rows 6-11 once **more**: 156 sts.

Row 28: K4, drop Blue; with second Blue, knit across.

Row 29: K4, drop Blue; with second Blue, purl across to last 4 sts, K4.

Size 9-12 Months Only

Rows 14-29: Repeat Rows 6-13 twice: 167 sts.

LOWER BODY

Row 1 (Dividing row)**:** Maintaining established stripe pattern, bands in Blue, and removing markers, K 20{23-25} (Front), slip next 30{35-38} sts onto st holder (Sleeve), **turn**; add on 4 sts for underarm, **turn**; K 35{40-41} (Back), slip next 30{35-38} sts onto st holder (Sleeve), **turn**; add on 4 sts for underarm, **turn**; knit across: 83{94-99} sts.

Row 2: K4, purl across to last 4 sts, K4.

Row 3: Knit across.

Repeat Rows 2 and 3 for pattern until Lower Body measures approximately 4½{4¾-5}"/11.5{12-12.5} cm from underarm **or** ¾" (1.9 cm) less than desired length ending by working a **wrong** side row and completing stripe; cut small ball of Blue.

Last 6 Rows: With next color, knit across.

Bind off all sts in **knit**.

SLEEVE

With **right** side facing, maintaining established stripe pattern, and using double pointed needle, pick up 4{3-4} sts across one underarm *(Fig. 13, page 46)*, place split ring marker around first st to indicate beginning of rnd; slip 10{11-12} sts from st holder onto opposite end of same needle and 10{12-13} sts onto each of 2 empty needles *(Fig. 1, page 44)*; knit around: 34{38-42} sts.

Working in established stripe pattern, knit each rnd until Sleeve measures approximately 3{4-5}"/7.5{10-12.5} cm **or** ¾" (1.9 cm) less than desired length from underarm, ending by completing stripe.

Next Rnd: With next color, purl around.

Next Rnd: Knit around.

Last 4 Rnds: Repeat last 2 rnds twice.

Bind off all sts in **purl**.

Repeat for remaining Sleeve.

Sew buttons to band opposite buttonholes.

GENERAL INSTRUCTIONS

ABBREVIATIONS

C4F	Cable 4 Front
cm	centimeters
K	knit
M1	make one
M1P	make one purl
mm	millimeters
P	purl
PSSO	pass slipped stitch over
P2SSO	pass 2 slipped stitches over
Rnd(s)	Round(s)
st(s)	stitch(es)
tog	together
YO	yarn over

SYMBOLS & TERMS

★ — work instructions following ★ as many **more** times as indicated in addition to the first time.

( ) or [ ] — work enclosed instructions **as many** times as specified by the number immediately following **or** contains explanatory remarks.

colon (:) — the number(s) given after a colon at the end of a row or round denote(s) the number of stitches you should have on that row or round.

GAUGE

Exact gauge is **essential** for proper fit. Before beginning your sweater, make a sample swatch in the yarn and needles specified in the individual instructions. After completing the swatch, measure it, counting your stitches and rows carefully. If your swatch is larger or smaller than specified, **make another, changing needle size to get the correct gauge.** Keep trying until you find the size needles that will give you the specified gauge.

KNIT TERMINOLOGY

UNITED STATES		INTERNATIONAL
gauge	=	tension
bind off	=	cast off
yarn over (YO)	=	yarn forward (yfwd) **or** yarn around needle (yrn)

KNITTING NEEDLES

U.S.	0	1	2	3	4	5	6	7	8	9	10	10½	11	13	15	17	19	35	50
U.K.	13	12	11	10	9	8	7	6	5	4	3	2	1	00	000	---	---	---	---
Metric - mm	2	2.25	2.75	3.25	3.5	3.75	4	4.5	5	5.5	6	6.5	8	9	10	12.75	15	19	25

■□□□ BEGINNER	Projects for first-time knitters using basic knit and purl stitches. Minimal shaping.
■■□□ EASY	Projects using basic stitches, repetitive stitch patterns, simple color changes, and simple shaping and finishing.
■■■□ INTERMEDIATE	Projects with a variety of stitches, such as basic cables and lace, simple intarsia, double-pointed needles and knitting in the round needle techniques, mid-level shaping and finishing.
■■■■ EXPERIENCED	Projects using advanced techniques and stitches, such as short rows, fair isle, more intricate intarsia, cables, lace patterns, and numerous color changes.

Yarn Weight Symbol & Names	LACE 0	SUPER FINE 1	FINE 2	LIGHT 3	MEDIUM 4	BULKY 5	SUPER BULKY 6
Type of Yarns in Category	Fingering, size 10 crochet thread	Sock, Fingering, Baby	Sport, Baby	DK, Light Worsted	Worsted, Afghan, Aran	Chunky, Craft, Rug	Bulky, Roving
Knit Gauge Range* in Stockinette St to 4" (10 cm)	33-40** sts	27-32 sts	23-26 sts	21-24 sts	16-20 sts	12-15 sts	6-11 sts
Advised Needle Size Range	000-1	1 to 3	3 to 5	5 to 7	7 to 9	9 to 11	11 and larger

*GUIDELINES ONLY: The chart above reflects the most commonly used gauges and needle sizes for specific yarn categories.

** Lace weight yarns are usually knitted on larger needles to create lacy openwork patterns. Accordingly, a gauge range is difficult to determine. Always follow the gauge stated in your pattern.

ZEROS

To consolidate the length of an involved pattern, zeros are sometimes used so that all sizes can be combined. For example, repeat Rows 6 and 7, 1{1-0} time(s) **more** means the first two sizes would repeat the rows once, and the largest size would do nothing.

MARKERS

As a convenience to you, we have used markers to help distinguish the beginning of a pattern or a round. Place markers as instructed. You may use purchased markers or tie a length of contrasting color yarn around the needle. When you reach a marker on each row or round, slip it from the left needle to the right needle or move a split ring marker up to first stitch; remove when no longer needed.

USING DOUBLE POINTED NEEDLES

When working too few stitches to use a circular needle, double pointed needles are required. Slip the stitches from the stitch holder as instructed onto each of 3 double pointed needles, forming a triangle. With the fourth needle, knit across the stitches on the first needle *(Fig. 1)*. You will now have an empty needle with which to knit the stitches from the next needle. Work the first stitch of each needle firmly to prevent gaps.

Fig. 1

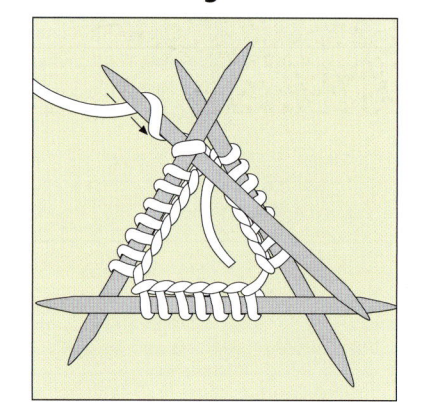

FOLLOWING A CHART

It is easier to follow a chart than written instructions and you can also see what the pattern looks like. The chart shows each stitch as a square indicating what color each stitch should be. Visualize the chart as your fabric, beginning at the bottom edge.

Only one pattern repeat is given on the chart, and it is indicated by a heavy vertical line and a bracketed indication. This section is to be repeated across the row. If the chart is symmetrical, it doesn't matter which direction the chart is followed. For ease in following the chart, place a ruler on the chart above the row being worked to help keep your place.

STRANDING

Stranding is the method in which the color not in use is carried across the **wrong** side of the fabric. It gives a nice appearance on the right side and also provides added warmth. Carry the yarn **loosely** across one to 4 sts, about 1" (2.5 cm) or less, without twisting the strands of yarn *(Fig. 2)*. Notice that each color is carried across the wrong side **without** crossing each other.

Fig. 2

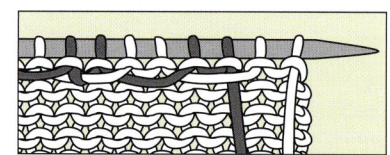

CHANGING COLORS

When changing colors, always pick up the new color yarn from **beneath** the dropped yarn and keep the color which has just been worked to the left *(Fig. 3)*. This will prevent holes in the finished piece. Take extra care to keep your tension even.

Fig. 3   Wrong side

INCREASES
INCREASING EVENLY ACROSS A ROW

Add one to the number of increases required and divide that number into the number of stitches on the needle. Subtract one from the result and the new number is the approximate number of stitches to be worked between each increase. Adjust the number as needed.

ADDING NEW STITCHES

Insert the right needle into stitch as if to **knit**, yarn over and pull loop through *(Fig. 4a)*, insert the left needle into the loop just worked from **front** to **back** and slip the loop onto the left needle *(Fig. 4b)*. Repeat for required number of stitches.

Fig. 4a

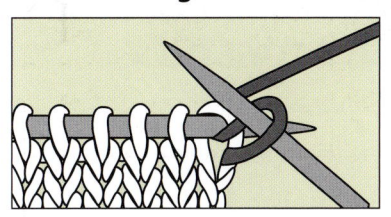

Fig. 4b

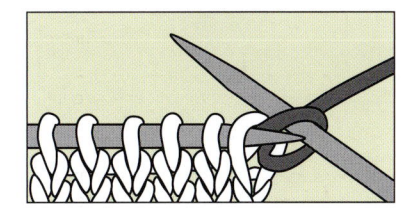

KNIT INCREASE

Knit the next stitch but do **not** slip the old stitch off the left needle *(Fig. 5a)*. Insert the right needle into the **back** loop of the **same** stitch and knit it *(Fig. 5b)*, then slip the old stitch off the left needle.

Fig. 5a

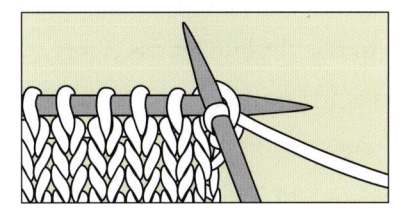

Fig. 5b

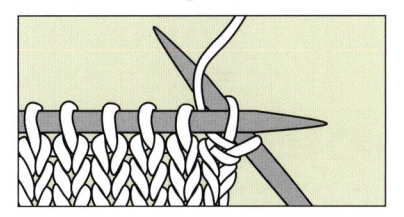

PURL INCREASE

Purl the next stitch but do **not** slip the old stitch off the left needle. Insert the right needle into the **back** loop of the **same** stitch from **back** to **front** *(Fig. 6)* and purl it. Slip the old stitch off the left needle.

Fig. 6

MAKE ONE *(abbreviated M1)*

Insert the **left** needle under the horizontal strand between the stitches from the front *(Fig. 7a)*. Then knit into the **back** of the strand *(Fig. 7b)*.

Fig. 7a

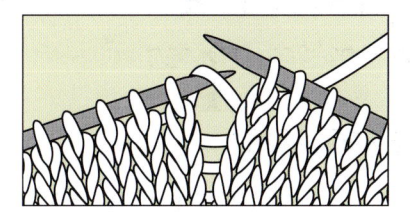

Fig. 7b

MAKE ONE PURL

(abbreviated M1P)

Insert the **left** needle under the horizontal strand between the stitches from the back *(Fig. 8a)*. Then purl into the **front** of the strand *(Fig. 8b)*.

Fig. 8a

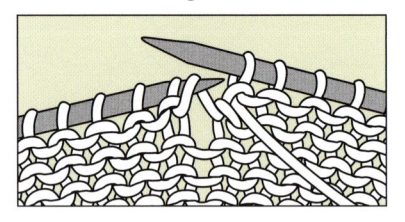

Fig. 8b

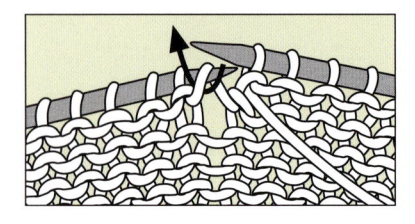

YARN OVER *(abbreviated YO)*

Bring the yarn forward **between** the needles, then back **over** the top of the right hand needle, so that it is now in position to knit the next stitch *(Fig. 9)*.

Fig. 9

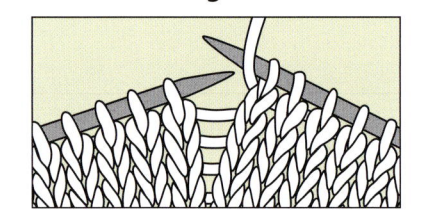

DECREASES
KNIT 2 TOGETHER

(abbreviated K2 tog)

Insert the right needle into the **front** of the first two stitches on the left needle as if to **knit** *(Fig. 10)*, then **knit** them together as if they were one stitch.

Fig. 10

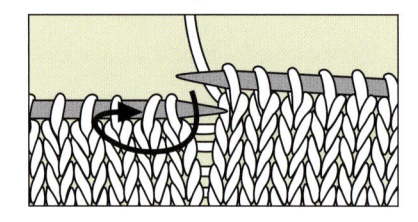

SLIP 1, KNIT 1, PASS SLIPPED STITCH OVER

(abbreviated slip 1, K1, PSSO)

Slip one stitch as if to **knit**. Knit the next stitch. With the left needle, bring the slipped stitch over the knit stitch *(Fig. 11)* and off the needle.

Fig. 11

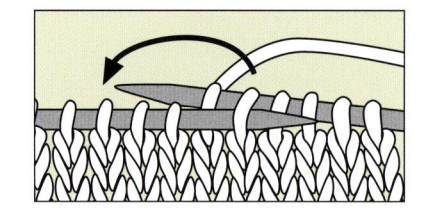

SLIP 2 TOGETHER, KNIT 1, PASS 2 SLIPPED STITCHES OVER

(abbreviated slip 2 tog, K1, P2SSO)

Slip next 2 stitches together as if to **knit** *(Fig. 12a)*. Knit the next stitch. With the left needle, bring the 2 slipped stitches over the stitch just made *(Fig. 12b)* and off the needle.

Fig. 12a

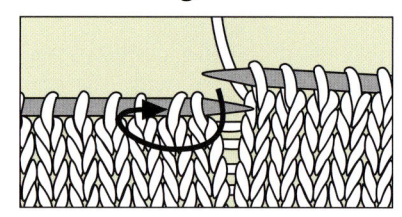

Fig. 12b

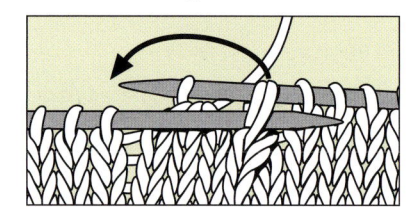

PICKING UP STITCHES

When instructed to pick up stitches, insert the needle from the **front** to the **back** under two strands at the edge of the worked piece *(Fig. 13)*. Put the yarn around the needle as if to **knit**, then bring the needle with the yarn back through the stitch to the right side, resulting in a stitch on the needle.

Repeat this along the edge, picking up the required number of stitches. A crochet hook may be helpful to pull yarn through.

Fig. 13

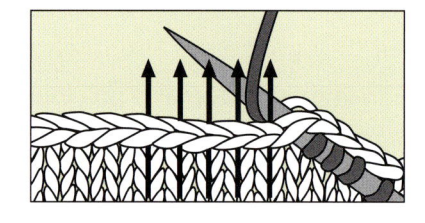

YARN INFORMATION

Each sweater in this book was made using Medium Weight Yarn. Any brand of Medium Weight Yarn may be used. It is best to refer to the yardage/meters when determining how many balls or skeins to purchase. Remember, to arrive at the finished size, it is the GAUGE/TENSION that is important, not the brand of yarn.

For your convenience, listed below are the specific yarns used to create our photography models. Because yarn manufacturers make frequent changes to their product lines, you may sometimes find it necessary to use a substitute yarn or to search for the discontinued product at alternate suppliers (locally or online).

CABLED EYELETS

Red Heart® With Love®

#1207 Cornsilk

EYELET LACE

Red Heart® With Love®

#1601 Lettuce

FAIR ISLE

Lion Brand® Vanna's Choice®

Grey Multi - #500 Patchwork Grey

Gold - #158 Mustard

Red - #113 Scarlet

HEARTS

Lion Brand® Vanna's Choice®

Grey - #401 Grey Marble

Red - #180 Cranberry

LEAVES

Lion Brand® Vanna's Choice®

#108 Dusty Blue

LATTICE LACE

Red Heart® With Love®

#1538 Lilac

WAVES

Red Heart® With Love®

#1805 Bluebell

ZIG-ZAG LACE

Red Heart® With Love®

#1711 Cameo

STRIPED

Lion Brand® Vanna's Choice®

Blue - #108 Dusty Blue

Lt Blue - #105 Silver Blue

Melissa Leapman

With more than 800 knit and crochet designs in print, Melissa Leapman is one of the most widely published American designers working today.

She began her design career by freelancing for leading ready-to-wear design houses in New York City. She also created designs to help top yarn companies promote their new and existing yarns each season. Her ability to quickly develop fully envisioned garments put her skills in great demand.

Through the years, Leisure Arts has published more than 40 books of Melissa's fabulous designs. Melissa is also the host of several Leisure Arts DVDs in the best-selling teach-yourself series, "I Can't Believe I'm Knitting" and "I Can't Believe I'm Crocheting."

Nationally, her designs have been featured in numerous magazines, and her workshops on knitting and crochet are consistently popular with crafters of all skill levels. She has taught at major events such as STITCHES, Vogue Knitting LIVE, and The Knitting Guild Association conferences, as well as at hundreds of yarn shops and local guild events across the country.

Look for other Leisure Arts books featuring Melissa's designs at www.leisurearts.com/meet-the-designers/melissa-leapman.html.

We have made every effort to ensure that these instructions are accurate and complete. We cannot, however, be responsible for human error, typographical mistakes, or variations in individual work.

Production Team: Instructional/ Technical Editor - Sarah J. Green; Senior Graphic Artist - Lora Puls; Graphic Artists - Amy L. Teeter and Maddy Ross; Photo Stylist - Lori Wenger; and Photographer - Jason Masters.

Copyright © 2019 by Leisure Arts, Inc., 104 Champs Blvd., STE 100, Maumelle, AR 72113-6738, www.leisurearts.com. All rights reserved. This publication is protected under federal copyright laws. Reproduction or distribution of this publication or any other Leisure Arts publication, including publications which are out of print, is prohibited unless specifically authorized. This includes, but is not limited to, any form of reproduction or distribution on or through the Internet, including posting, scanning, or e-mail transmission.

Made in U.S.A.